Spirit Around The Sound

by Shirley Shadbolt

Copyright 2008 by Shirley Shadbolt. All rights reserved.

ISBN 978-0-6152-0609-7

Published by Shirley Shadbolt

For Ron for believing in me.

Contents

Where Mighty Rivers Flow..6

Sauk Mountain Climb...9

A Memorial Weekend..13

Beneath The Ice Cream Cone..16

I Remember The Earthquake..19

The Fall..23

Widow's Web...25

Flight Of A Widow's Love..27

Behind The Smile...29

The Other Side of Summer..31

Into The Pale Moonlight...33

Love Changes Everything..35

Steel Dreams..38

A Wild Goose Chase..40

I Love My Sweats...42

Pet Peeve..44

Where I Belong...47

Because You Cared For Me...52

WHERE MIGHTY RIVERS FLOW

I live in a land where mighty rivers flow.

Listen carefully as I say their names;

Consist of splendid words you may like to know.

Most begin high in the North Cascade Range.

They're called the Nooksack, Samish,

Skykomish, Snohomish, and Stillaguamish.

Then of course there's the Snoqualimie.

O' but, the magnificent Skagit runs past me!

She joins upstream forming her own system.

It includes the Sauk, Suiattle, and Cascade.

Merging together binding mountains to the sea;

Emerald ribbons showing off their majesty.

She winds down steep slopes always restless.

Through forested hillsides and wide valleys.

She rises and falls past rugged wilderness,

Farmlands, cities, and rural communities.

Ebb and flow of her moving waters influences lives;

Revealed in wildlife; deer, black bear, mountain goat,

Grizzlies, grey wolves, bald eagles and bull trout.

Farmlands rich with fertile soil, and countless fisheries.

What marvelous treasures our forefathers must have found,

Amongst the rivers and tributaries above Puget Sound!

The mighty Skagit River System is still called home,

To four Native American Indian Tribes in this poem.

Listen closely as I say their names~

The Upper Skagit,

Sauk-Suiattle,

Samish,

and Swinomish.

Sauk Mountain Climb

Out front of me,

Sauk Mountain looms.

She beckons brilliantly.

Radiating gorgeous blooms.

Mounting adventurous thoughts,

Below her majesty.

Surrendering alas I sought,

What treasures awaited me.

Ever climb a mountain

When you're past your prime?

Well I proved you can;

Last summer I climbed mine.

Along narrow paths ahead,

Lie meadows of wildflowers.

Breathtaking beauty left unsaid,

Leading up to rocky towers.

Trudging up steep switchbacks,

Water pouring off my face.

Apple juice came out my pack,

Much needed in this race.

Breathlessly I reached the top,

What panoramic view.

T'was there I made my resting stop,

Before descending down anew.

Coming down should be a breeze.

Least you think it true;

Excruciating pain within my knees

Began without a clue.

Wincing every rocking step.

Knowing exactly what to do,

Gathering up my trophies crept,

Clutching fingers turning blue.

A Memorial Weekend

May eighteenth of nineteen eighty,

A dormant mountain came alive.

Exploding boiling mud and ash,

Fifty-seven victims did not survive.

Sadly most lost their life that day,

Because officials failed to foresee;

The scale of the disaster area,

Inside the 'Red Zone'- only three.

Trees lay flattened on the ground,

Seventeen miles from the crater.

Mt. St. Helens sent plumes of ash,

Blocking out the sun hours later.

Volcanic ash began falling like snow,

Reaching Montana at a surprising rate.

Measuring a wide catastrophic scope,

From a major eruption in another state.

Two weeks passed before our invite.

Convinced now we had nothing to fear,

Loaded our camper and packed our crew,

For Memorial Day in Oregon that year.

About halfway white stuff began falling.

Seems St.Helens wasn't through yet.

Finally we arived outside of Portland,

Ash covered everything like a blanket.

Sought refuge inside during the entire visit.

Drove back through ash along the I-5 strip.

Plastic bags filled up served as souvenirs.

We'll never forget our memorable trip!

Beneath The Ice Cream Cone

Living near the North Cascades,

brings not just joy but fears.

Mt. Baker rises above me,

an active volcano for years.

She dominates the skyline

in Washington from Bellingham

to British Colombia, above the alpine.

Just eighteen miles from where I am.

With her glaciers heavily sprawled,

she's one of the snowiest places in the world.

"The Ice Cream Cone" she's called.

Our future uncertainty resides below,

resulting from her eruptive past.

History shows one pyroclastic flow

occuring thousands of years ago,

coming from a lateral blast.

Last known destruction facts refer-

back to the middle eighteen hundreds,

when tephra eruptions caused lava flows

and mud flows, which still remain

this volcano's largest hazard.

On clear cold winter days

steam plumes rise from her craters,

alarming all who live around here,

mindful ever for some warning.

We rely on US Geological Surveys

to monitor our mountain's activities.

Who under "The Ice Cream Cone" really relaxes?

Certainty? In this world nothing

is certain but death and taxes.

Or is it?

I Remember the Earthquake

The quaking earth below

delivered her fateful body blow.

Registering a magnitude 6.8

on the seismic Richter Scale.

When all shaking stopped,

we looked around to know,

Extent of all the damage

which had turned our faces pale.

Our precious Northwest home

now stood ripped apart;

Shattering a shaken couple,

slowly picking up the pieces.

Devastating stresses proved

too much for a failing heart;

Lost my partner within days

in spite of cardiac devices.

Suddenly, I'm on my own

drifting into empty dazes.

Watching crews spend hours

repairing roof and foundation.

Wondering, how-who- would fix

this widow's hollow gazes?

Friends and family rallied round

supporting my condition.

Months of loneliness went by

reminding me of buried vows.

How on earth could I survive

what lies ahead without him?

Then one day I joined an

online club for widowers and widows.

Thoughts of ever finding

partnership again seemed so dim.

Unknowingly, across PugetSound's waters

a lonely widower awaited.

Seems, he had lost his beloved

several days before the rumbling.

Months had passed without her,

leaving a home life feeling slated.

Giving into desire, he found

an online club above his humbling.

Unaware of his yearning,

I cried out in finale desperation:

"Dear God help me get through this,

give me strength to see it through"

in my email came this message

typed in bold uppercase dictation:

"I REMEMBER THE EARTHQUAKE TOO"

THE FALL

October chill is in my room.

I awake alone in darkness;

Reaching for your pillow;

Pulling it close to me;

Pulverizing it with frustrated fists.

I cry out desperately-

"Oh God"!

What is happening to my identity?

Bring me back the soul

That is slipping from me.

Make me whole again.

For I yearn for peace of mind,

That once was mine.

Oh, and I wonder in bleakness;

In the chill of my bedroom.

Where is my sanity?

Widow's Web

Vivid dreams of bygone days,

Frequent night time visions.

Retiring alone she lays,

Sinking fitfully in her prisons.

~She is spinning

Morning breaks another day,

Scattering overhanging silence.

Mundane chores get underway,

Blocking memories of glances.

~She is spinning

Pacing emptiness away,

Chases ever present redolence's.

Should she leave, should she stay?

Ponders constant loneliness.

~She is spinning

Seeking pleasures flown,

She's searching her identity.

Circling friendships on her own,

She's trying to capture infinity.

~She is waiting

Flight of a Widow's Love

Where are you darling?

Spring has arrived with much mating.

This has not caused me sorrow.

You have shown me real love,

With passion and compassion.

Our love will never die.

It will go on you'll see.

I saw two little birds that flew,

Into the big fir tree;

Chattering their love song to each other.

Then the male he flew out of the tree,

To come and sit upon my fence.

She was still up in the tree

Chirp, chirp, chirping for him.

Then they both flew up

Into the air together.

They danced their love dance

Between the big fir

And the alder.

Behind the Smile

He arrived late one summer eve

Peering out from behind shrubbery

At first glance, I could perceive

How his smile set me free.

Peering out from behind shrubbery

Beaming approval, crushing all appall

How his smile set me free

Breaking down longstanding walls.

Beaming approval, crushing all appall

Curiosity prompted me to consider

Breaking down longstanding walls

Banishing rejection- that left me bitter.

Curiosity prompted me to consider

At first glance, I did perceive

Banishing rejection- that left me bitter

He arrived late one summer eve.

~A Pantoum Poem

The Other Side of Summer

Overwhelming sorrow and grief

Rained down amongst summer heat.

Lives torn apart one fleeting instant

Left faltering alone in disbelief.

Longer days bring fading images

Burning memories of you and me.

Sole fueling embers of quiet rage

Knowing we can no longer be.

Reaching out for Divine rapture

Reversed our fate and set us free.

Allowing broken hearts to capture

Long summer nights of ecstasy.

INTO THE PALE MOONLIGHT

You'll find me forever walking this street.

Undying love leaves me no choice.

'Twas here that so long ago we'd meet.

Our forbidden love had no voice.

Seems your heart was already spoken for.

Mine hanging onto a fleeting passion.

Woefully, willingly, I was your whore.

Knowing you may leave after a fashion.

Slipping past rocks we'd make our way,

To the seashore and make love in the sand.

Allowing emotions to sweep us away,

Giving into our savage demands.

Proving then you would never claim me,

Opened my eyes in the pale moonlight.

This time I had come to set you free;

You'd be marrying another the next night.

Years find me yearning for lost love,

Always wondering if you remember me.

Strolling, I find myself looking above,

At the balcony where you used to be.

Every night since, I come back alone,

And wander down Turnberry Street.

Seeking to capture a love that has flown,

Perhaps in another lifetime we'll meet.

Love Changes Everything

True love came calling,

Later in years,

And we found,

Our selves swept off our feet.

Blinded by passion,

Fueling embers,

That smoldered forever it seems.

Tasting our sweetness,

Catching our breath,

Chasing our wildest dream.

Letting it carry us,

Far over the rainbow,

Never bringing us back again.

Miles from where

We started out;

We remained

Set in our old ways.

Seems now...

There's no turning back.

We were so blind;

How could we have known?

Love changes everything!

Steel Dreams

Fall arrived nipping at crisp clean air,

Splattering patches of blue skies above.

So we slipped into nylon liners to wear,

Underneath our black leather gloves.

Our jackets zipped with quilted thermal.

We filled our boots with heavy wool socks.

Warmer riding gear- now the normal,

Soon we'll be turning back our clocks.

We're riding tandem today on the Vulcan,

We're trying to capture our youth so it seems.

A couple of coldblooded aging Americans,

Flying high with the thrill of our Steel Dream's.

A Wild Goose Chase

Pulled up to my ole fishing hole,
It was one hot day down at the lake.
Popped the trunk to find my pole,
T'was then I did a double take.

Out from amongst the tallest reed,
The big goose waddled straight
For me- still his bill I did not heed;
I turned instead to choose my bait.

Closer now feathers began to ruffle.
He straightened out his skinny neck.
His honking sounds made me scuffle;
I knew bare legs might feel a peck.

My quest on hold for fishing gear,
I began the chase without thinking.
I chased that goose without a fear!
Soon found myself in sand sinking.

Suddenly he reared his head high.
He hissed loudly- beak opened wide.
Ouch! He bit me hard upon my thigh;
Leaving his reminder I cannot hide.

I Love My Sweats

I get them for my birthday,

Some at Christmas time.

Perhaps this Mother's Day,

They'll be a wish of mine.

They come in different colors,

Some with a pastel hue.

My favorite pair is yellow,

Yet I've been seen in blue.

I wear the fleece in winter,

When it's freezing cold outside.

Now I don't have to shiver,

For I've set my jeans aside.

Sweats are soft and loose,

Around my waist they fit.

Those denims wore a noose,

Across my crotch when'er I sit.

I wear them in morning,

And in evening too.

They don't require ironing,

My wardrobe's less to do.

Imagine being without them,

Not on your life it's true.

They've become a real gem,

At my age, how 'bout you?

Pet Peeve

What words abound

To serve me best

To write a poem

About my pet?

That it could

Succeed to be

Perfect in eyes

Of all the rest.

Not just some

Relentless boring tale

Of ones own

Furry pleasure-stale.

How can I

Make the reader

Connect to feline

Antics they beset?

Or convince them

How adorably fine

An ugly canine is

Is of mine?

Perplexed, I seek

To end vexation

Make plain resolve

Of this pet situation.

I'll do my best

To make them see

How precious pets

Can really be.

Perhaps improve

More vivid imagery

With hope to move

Their empathy.

Putting to rest

What some perceive

Each time I write

Of such pet peeve!

Where I Belong

When Gaby asked me,

this was her plea-

"Shi, will you run a

workshop for me?"

Without hesitation

I did agree.

Then set out to make it

the best it could be.

Carefully, choosing

my topic with glee-

Narrative Poetry is what

I decided it should be;

excluding Ballad and Epic,

limited time was the key.

So I set out gathering

all information I could,

and began the formatting

so each member understood.

My group would consist

of five members and me.

My job was to assist;

what they would learn-

no guarantee.

My workshop was scheduled

one week in February.

For months I assembled

everything necessary.

All of a sudden,

my turn had come;

my stomach tightened.

I had no where to run!

I was frozen and frightened.

How could this be?

I never imagined

it could happen to me!

All of these doubts

and fears rushed through

my head- I wanted to shout

"I'm not a teacher!

I haven't a clue!"

"What on earth am I doing

in this group with you?"

Then much to my amazement

poems began coming in.

Magnificent accomplishments

bringing forth great big grins.

Stirring up emotions

deep down inside.

My heart filled and

nearly burst with pride!

Calmly my doubts

finally disappeared,

enthralled by these

gifted writers' words.

Unknowingly, they banished

all I had feared

as my heart sang to

music of their magical chords

I knew in an instant

I was where I belonged.

Because You Cared For Me

I sailed around
the world wide,
searching from
sea to sea.
Then our ships
they did collide.

Our love was meant to be.

I climbed the highest
mountain peak.
Reached down and
found the way to free
those words of love
I dared not speak,

Because you cared for me.

Finally, I conquered
all my fears,
and watched my
sorrow flee,
as you gently wiped
away my tears,

Because you cared for me.

www.ingramcontent.com/pod-product-compliance
Lightning Source LLC
Chambersburg PA
CBHW041702160426
43202CB00002B/12